Roots

By

Steffi Cavell-Clarke

©2017
Book Life
King's Lynn
Norfolk PE30 4LS

ISBN: 978-1-78637-149-2

Written by:
Steffi Cavell-Clarke

Edited by:
Charlie Ogden

Designed by:
Danielle Jones

A catalogue record for this book
is available from the British Library

PHOTO CREDITS

Supporting Learning in Schools

Roots

CONTENTS

BeetROOT!

growing underground

Words that look like **this** can be found in the glossary on page 24.

What Is a Plant?

A plant is a living thing. All living things need water, air and **sunlight** to live.

There are many different kinds of plant. Most plants have roots, leaves, flowers and a stem.

Plants live all around the world!

5

What Are Roots?

There are some plants that don't have any roots!

Roots are the part of a plant that usually **grow** downwards into the **soil**.

Roots are very important. They **absorb** water and **nutrients** from the soil that the plant can use.

What Do Roots Look Like?

Roots come in many different shapes, sizes and colours. They usually grow underground, which makes them difficult to see.

Some roots are very big, but others are much smaller.

The roots of an oak tree can grow over eight metres long!

9

How Do Roots Grow?

When a seed has enough water and warmth from the sun, it will grow a root.

As a plant grows, it keeps growing more roots.

Some orchids' roots grow upwards as they absorb water from the air.

There are other types of plant that grow roots above the ground.

Mistletoe grows on trees. Its roots break into the tree's **bark** and share the tree's nutrients.

13

What Do Roots Do?

Roots that grow downwards into the soil absorb water and nutrients.

The water and nutrients move up the plant's stem and into the leaves.

Soil

Nutrients

Roots

Water

15

16

Leaves need water in order to make food for the plant. They get the water they need from the roots.

Without roots, a plant could be blown over by the wind.

17

Plants Without **Roots**

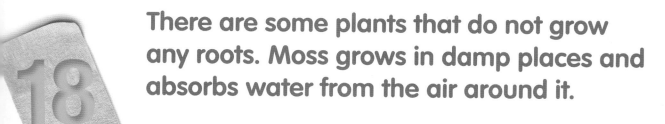

There are some plants that do not grow any roots. Moss grows in damp places and absorbs water from the air around it.

Seaweed has **holdfasts** instead of roots. Holdfasts help the seaweed to grow on the sea bed, but they do not take in water or nutrients.

Seaweed

19

Roots in the Forest

Sometimes you can see big roots growing into soil!

There are many trees in a **forest**. Lots of trees have big, thick roots that go deep underground.

Very large trees have thick roots that hold the tree in place. Large trees need to soak up more water and nutrients than small trees.

21

Tasty Roots

There are some roots that are safe for humans to eat. They are called root vegetables.

Carrots are roots because they grow underground!

23

GLOSSARY

absorb soak up
bark a tough layer on the outside of trees
forests areas of land covered in trees
grow naturally develop and increase in size
holdfasts root-like structures that hold seaweed in place
nutrients natural substances that plants need to grow
soil the upper layer of earth where plants grow
sunlight light from the sun

INDEX